D1574459

PIZZA PARTY COOKBOOK

THE WORLD'S FAVORITE PIZZA RECIPES

BY HOMEMADE PIZZA MAKER

© Copyright 2020 by _Homemade Pizza Maker - All rights reserved.

The following Book is reproduced below to provide information that is as accurate and reliable as possible. Regardless, purchasing this Book can be seen as consent because both the Publisher and the author of this book are in no way experts on the topics discussed within. Any recommendations or suggestions that are made herein are for entertainment purposes only. Professionals should be consulted as needed prior to undertaking any of the actions endorsed herein.

This declaration is deemed fair and valid by both the American Bar Association and the Committee of Publishers Association and is legally binding throughout the United States.

Furthermore, the transmission, duplication, or reproduction of any of the following work, including specific information, will be considered an illegal act irrespective of if it is done electronically or in print. This extends to creating a secondary or tertiary copy of the work or a recorded copy and is only allowed with the Publisher's express written consent. All additional rights reserved.

The information in the following pages is broadly considered a truthful and accurate account of facts. As such, any inattention, use, or misuse of the information in question by the reader will render any resulting actions solely under their purview. There are no scenarios in which the Publisher or the original author of this work can be in any fashion deemed liable for any hardship or damages that may befall them after undertaking information described herein.

Additionally, the following pages' information is intended only for informational purposes and should thus be thought of as universal. As befitting its nature, it is presented without assurance regarding its prolonged validity or interim quality. Trademarks that are mentioned are done without written consent and can in no way be considered an endorsement from the trademark holder.

TABLE OF CONTENTS

Pizza Dough

Ingredients

- 1 (.25 ounce) package active dry yeast
- 1 cup warm water (110 degrees F/45 degrees C)
- 2 cups bread flour
- 2 tablespoons olive oil 1 teaspoon salt
- 2 teaspoons white sugar

Directions

In a small bowl, dissolve yeast in warm water. Let stand until creamy, about 10 minutes.

In a large bowl, combine 2 cups bread flour, olive oil, salt, white sugar, and the yeast mixture; stir well to combine. Beat well until a stiff dough has formed. Cover and rise until doubled in volume, about 30 minutes. Meanwhile, preheat the oven to 350 degrees F (175 degrees C).

Turn dough out onto a well-floured surface. Form dough into a round and roll out into a pizza crust shape. Cover with your favorite sauce and toppings and bake in the preheated oven until golden brown, about 20 minutes.

Artichoke and Shrimp Alfredo Pizza

Ingredients

- 1 teaspoon olive oil
- 1/2-pound uncooked large shrimp, peeled and deveined
- 1/8 teaspoon crushed red pepper flakes
- (12 inches) prebaked pizza crust
- 3/4 cup Bertolli® Creamy Alfredo Sauce
- (14 ounces) jar marinated artichoke hearts, drained
- tablespoons chopped drained sun-dried tomatoes packed in oil
- 1/3 cup shredded mozzarella cheese

Directions

Preheat oven to 450 degrees F.

Heat olive oil in a 10-inch nonstick skillet over medium-high heat and cook shrimp with red pepper flakes, turning once, 2 minutes, or until shrimp turn pink.

Arrange pizza crust on an ungreased baking sheet. Evenly top with 1/2 cup sauce, then artichokes, tomatoes, and cooked shrimp. Top with remaining sauce, then sprinkle with cheese. Bake 12 minutes or until cheese is melted.

Pizza Salad

Ingredients

- 1 (16 ounces) package small shell pasta
- 1 red bell pepper, chopped
- 1 green bell pepper, chopped
- 1 tomato, chopped
- 5 green onions, chopped
- 1 (4.5 ounces) can sliced mushrooms, drained
- 2 1/2 ounces sliced pepperoni sausage
- 1 (2.25 ounce) can slice black olives, drained
- 2 cloves garlic, minced
- 1 teaspoon dried oregano
- 1/2 teaspoon salt
- 1/4 teaspoon ground black pepper
- 1 cup Italian-style salad dressing
- 1 cup shredded mozzarella cheese
- 2 tablespoons grated Parmesan cheese

Directions

In a large pot of salted boiling water, cook pasta until al dente, rinse under cold water and drain.

In a large bowl, combine the pasta, red bell pepper, green bell pepper, tomato, green onions, mushrooms, pepperoni, olives, garlic, oregano, salt, and pepper. Toss together and refrigerate until chilled.

Before serving, add dressing and cheese; mix together well.

Bubble Pizza

Ingredients

- 1 pound ground beef
- 1/4-pound sliced pepperoni sausage
- 1 (14 ounces) pizza sauce
- 1 (12 ounce) packages refrigerated buttermilk biscuit dough
- 1/2 onion, sliced and separated into rings
- 1 (10 ounces) can slice black olives
- 1 (4.5 ounces) can sliced mushrooms
- 1 1/2 cups shredded mozzarella cheese
- 1 cup shredded Cheddar cheese

Directions

Preheat oven to 400 degrees F (200 degrees C). Grease a 9x13 inch baking dish. Place ground beef in a large, deep skillet. Cook over medium-high heat until evenly brown. Stir in pepperoni and cook until browned. Drain excess fat. Stir in pizza sauce. Remove from heat and set aside.

Cut biscuits into quarters, and place them in the bottom of the baking dish. Spread the meat mixture evenly over the biscuits. Sprinkle top with onion, olives, and mushrooms.

Bake uncovered in preheated oven for 20 to 25 minutes. Sprinkle top with mozzarella and Cheddar cheese. Bake an additional 5 to 10 minutes until cheese is melted. Let stand 10 minutes before serving.

Canadian Bacon Pizza

Ingredients

- 1 (1 pound) loaf French bread
- 1/4 cup butter, melted
- 2 cups marinara sauce
- 16 slices Canadian bacon
- 1 (20 ounces) can unsweeten pineapple tidbits, drained
- 1/2 cup chopped green pepper
- 1/4 cup chopped green onions 2 cups shredded mozzarella cheese

Directions

Cut bread in half lengthwise, then in half widthwise. Place cut side up in a foil-lined 15-in. x 10-in. x 1-in. baking pan. Brush with butter. Bake at 450 degrees F for 5 minutes or until lightly browned.

Spread marinara sauce over bread. Top with Canadian bacon, pineapple, green pepper, onions, and cheese.

Bake for 8-10 minutes or until cheese is melted. Cut each piece in half.

Pizza al Forno

Ingredients

- 1/2 cup Bertolli® Creamy Alfredo Sauce
- 1/2 cup ricotta cheese
- 1 (12 inches) prebaked pizza crust
- 2 plum tomatoes, thinly sliced
- 4 ounces fresh mozzarella cheese, thinly sliced

Directions

Preheat oven to 425 degrees F.

Combine sauce with ricotta in a medium bowl.

Arrange pizza crust on an ungreased pizza pan or baking sheet. Evenly spread with ricotta mixture, then top with tomatoes and mozzarella cheese.

Bake 15 minutes or until the ricotta mixture is bubbling. Garnish, if desired, with Parmesan cheese curls and fresh basil leaves.

Sausage Cheeseburger Pizza

Ingredients

- 1 (1 pound) package Bob Evans® Original Recipe Sausage Roll
- 1 (12-inch) prepared pizza crust
- 1/2 cup yellow mustard
- 2 cups shredded mozzarella cheese
- 1/2 cup chopped onions
- 15 dill pickle slices
- 3/4 cup shredded Cheddar cheese

Directions

Preheat oven to 425 degrees F. Crumble and cook sausage in a medium skillet until browned; drain well on paper towels. Place pizza dough on a lightly greased 12-inch pizza pan or baking sheet. Spread mustard over dough; top with mozzarella cheese, sausage, and onions. Place pickle slices evenly on top; sprinkle with cheddar cheese. Bake 12 minutes or until crust is cooked through and cheese is bubbly. Cut into thin wedges or squares and serve hot.

Refrigerate leftovers.

Garlic Chicken Pizza

Ingredients

- 1 1/8 cups warm water (110 degrees F/45 degrees C)
- 1 1/4 teaspoons salt
- 1 1/2 teaspoons vegetable oil
- 3 cups bread flour
- 2 tablespoons dry milk powder
- 2 teaspoons active dry yeast
- 2 tablespoons cornmeal
- 1 cup roasted garlic and parmesan cheese sauce
- 1/4 teaspoon granulated garlic
- 10 ounces mozzarella cheese, shredded
- 2 grilled skinless, boneless chicken breast, diced
- 1/4 red onion, sliced
- 1 tomato, cut into thin wedges
- 1 green bell pepper, seeded and diced

Directions

Place ingredients in the pan of the bread machine in the order recommended by the manufacturer. Select dough cycle; press Start.

Preheat oven to 475 degrees F (245 degrees C). Sprinkle a large pizza pan with cornmeal. Roll or pat dough out on a lightly floured surface until it is the pizza pan's diameter; place on pan.

Spread dough with sauce, then sprinkle with garlic. Cover with cheese. On top of the pizza, arrange chicken, green pepper, onion, and tomato.

Bake in preheated oven for 20 to 25 minutes, or until dough is baked, cheese is melted, and toppings are lightly browned.

Spaghetti Pizza

Ingredients

- 1 (8 ounces) package spaghetti
- 1 pound ground beef
- 2 1/2 cups spaghetti sauce
- 1/2 cup grated Parmesan cheese
- 2 eggs, beaten
- 3 slices processed American cheese
- 1 (8 ounces) package shredded mozzarella cheese

Directions

Preheat oven to 350 degrees F (175 degrees C).

Bring a large pot of lightly salted water to a boil. Add pasta and cook for 8 to 10 minutes or until al dente; drain.

Meanwhile, place ground beef in a large, deep skillet. Cook over medium-high heat until evenly brown. Drain, crumble and combine with spaghetti sauce.

In a large bowl, toss pasta with Parmesan cheese and eggs. Press into a 9-inch pie plate and spread the sauce mixture over pasta. Top with American cheese and sprinkle with mozzarella.

Bake in preheated oven for 30 minutes. Let stand 5 minutes before cutting into wedges.

Chicago-Style Pan Pizza

Ingredients

- 1 (1 pound) loaf frozen bread dough, thawed
- 1 pound bulk Italian sausage
- 2 cups shredded mozzarella cheese
- 8 ounces sliced fresh mushrooms 1 small onion, chopped
- 2 teaspoons olive oil
- 1 (28 ounces) can diced tomatoes, drained
- 3/4 teaspoon dried oregano
- 1/2 teaspoon salt
- 1/4 teaspoon fennel seed
- 1/4 teaspoon garlic powder
- 1/2 cup freshly grated Parmesan cheese

Directions

Preheat the oven to 350 degrees F (175 degrees C).
Press the dough into the bottom and up the sides of a greased 9x13 inch baking dish.

Crumble the sausage into a large skillet over medium-high heat. Cook and stir until evenly browned. Remove the link with a slotted spoon, and sprinkle over the dough crust. Sprinkle mozzarella cheese evenly over the sausage.

Add mushrooms and onion to the skillet; cook and stir until the onion is tender. Stir in the tomatoes, oregano, salt, fennel seed, and garlic powder. Spoon over the mozzarella cheese. Sprinkle Parmesan cheese over the top.

Bake for 25 to 35 minutes in the preheated oven or until the crust is golden brown.

Chicken Salsa Pizza

Ingredients

- 1 (14 ounces) package prebaked Italian bread shell crust
- 2 cups shredded Cheddar cheese, divided
- 1 (12 ounces) jar salsa
- 1 cup cubed cooked chicken

Directions

Place bread shell on an ungreased 12-in. pizza pan. Sprinkle with 3/4 cup of cheese. Top with salsa, chicken, and remaining cheese. Bake at 450 degrees F for 8-10 minutes or until cheese is bubbly.

Mexican Pizza

Ingredients

- 1 (16 ounces) can refry beans 1 pound ground beef
- 1 (1.25 ounce) package taco seasoning mix
- 1 tablespoon vegetable oil
- 4 (6 inches) corn tortillas
- 8 ounces shredded Cheddar cheese
- 8 tablespoons sour cream
- 2 roma (plum) tomatoes, chopped
- 2 green onion, chopped
- 1 (4 ounces) can dice green chiles, drained
- 1/2 avocado, diced
- 1 tablespoon black olives, sliced

Directions

Heat the refried beans.

In a large skillet, brown the ground beef. Stir in the seasoning packet.

Preheat oven to 350 degrees F (175 degrees C).

Place a small amount of vegetable oil in a large skillet. Let the oil heat, then place one corn tortilla in the skillet. After 15 seconds, flip the tortilla over and let it fry another 15 seconds. Repeat this process with the remaining tortillas, letting them drain on paper towels once they have been heated. When the tortillas have drained, arrange them on a cookie sheet.

Spread a thin layer of beans on the tortillas, followed by a beef and cheese layer.

Bake the tortillas in the preheated oven for 20 to 30 minutes. Slice the tortillas into wedges, arrange them on plates or a serving platter, and garnish them with sour cream, tomatoes, green onions, chiles, avocado, and olives.

Potato Pizza Casserole

Ingredients

- 1 pound ground beef
- 1 small onion, chopped salt, and pepper to taste
- 1/4 teaspoon garlic powder
- 5 cups peeled and thinly sliced potatoes
- 1 (3 ounces) package chopped pepperoni
- 1 (10.75 ounces) can condensed tomato soup
- 1 (10.75 ounces) can condensed Cheddar cheese soup
- 1/2 cup milk
- 1/2 teaspoon dried oregano
- 1/4 teaspoon Italian seasoning
- 1/2 teaspoon brown sugar
- 8 ounces shredded mozzarella cheese

Directions

Preheat the oven to 350 degrees F (175 degrees C). Cook the ground beef and onion in a large skillet over medium heat until evenly browned. Drain off grease—season with salt, pepper, and garlic powder.

Spread the sliced potatoes in a layer on the bottom of a 9x13 inch baking dish. Spread the ground beef and onion over the potatoes—place slices of pepperoni over the ground beef. In a saucepan over medium heat, combine the tomato soup, Cheddar cheese soup, and milk. Season with oregano, Italian seasoning, and brown sugar. Mix well, and cook until heated through. Pour over the contents of the baking dish.

Cover the dish with aluminum foil, and bake for 30 minutes in the preheated oven. Remove the aluminum foil, sprinkle mozzarella cheese over the top, and bake for an additional 15 minutes until the cheese is melted and bubbly.

Pizzalike

Ingredients

- 2 pounds ground beef
- 1 medium onion, chopped
- 2 (10.75 ounces) cans condensed tomato soup, undiluted
- 1 teaspoon dried oregano
- 1 teaspoon chili powder
- 1/2 teaspoon garlic salt
- 1 cup shredded Cheddar cheese
- 1 cup shredded mozzarella cheese
- 12 hamburger buns, split
- 1 tablespoon butter or margarine, melted

Directions

In a large skillet, cook beef and onion over medium heat until meat is no longer pink; drain. Stir in the soup, oregano, chili powder, and garlic salt. Bring to a boil. Remove from the heat; stir in cheeses.

Place about 1/3 cup meat mixture on each bun. Brush tops of buns with butter. Place on an ungreased baking sheet. Bake at 375 degrees F for 7-9 minutes or until cheese is melted. Or wrap sandwiches in foil and freeze for up to 3 months.

To bake frozen sandwiches: Place foil-wrapped buns on an ungreased baking sheet. Bake at 375 degrees F for 35-40 minutes or until heated through.

Duck and Fontina Pizza With Rosemary

Ingredients

- 1 large skin-on, boneless duck breast half
- 1 small yellow onion, sliced
- 1 tablespoon olive oil
- 2 tablespoons honey
- 1 (8 ounces) tub spreadable goat cheese
- 1 (10 ounces) package prebaked pizza crust
- salt and pepper to taste
- 10 ounces fontina cheese, shredded
- 1 tablespoon dried rosemary

Directions

Preheat oven to 450 degrees F (230 degrees C).

Cut several slits into the duck breast's fatty skin in a skillet over medium heat, fry skin-side-down for 10 minutes. Flip and continue to cook in its own fat for 10 minutes more. Remove from pan. Carefully remove the skin using a sharp knife, then slice and set aside.

Meanwhile, in a separate skillet, cook onions in olive oil over medium heat until translucent and soft, about 5 minutes. Mix in honey and continue to cook until brown and fragrant, 5 to 7 minutes more.

Spread goat cheese evenly over pizza crust and season with salt and pepper. Then layer with caramelized onions, fontina cheese, duck breast slices, and rosemary.

Bake in the preheated oven until cheese in the pizza center is completely melted, about 10 minutes.

Awesome Barbeque Chicken Pizza

Ingredients

- 1 tablespoon sesame oil
- 1 skinless, boneless chicken breast half
- 1/4 cup barbeque sauce, divided
- 1/2 cup marinara sauce
- 1 (16 ounces) package prebaked pizza crust
- 1 cup shredded mozzarella cheese
- 1/3 cup thinly sliced red onion
- 2 tablespoons chopped fresh cilantro

Directions

Heat the sesame oil in a skillet over medium heat. Place the chicken breast in the skillet and top with 1 tablespoon barbeque sauce.

Cook 10 minutes, turn, and top with 1 tablespoon barbeque sauce. Continue cooking for 10 minutes until juices run clear. Cool slightly, and cut into chunks.

Preheat oven to 425 degrees F (220 degrees C).

In a small bowl, mix the remaining barbeque sauce and marinara sauce. Spread evenly over the pizza crust. Sprinkle with mozzarella cheese. Arrange cooked chicken chunks and red onion slices over the top.

Bake 15 minutes in the preheated oven or until cheese is melted and bubbly. Remove from heat, sprinkle with cilantro, and let sit 10 minutes before slicing.

Pizza Burgers

Ingredients

- 1 (6 ounces) can tomato paste
- 1/2 teaspoon salt
- 1/2 teaspoon dried oregano
- 1/4 teaspoon garlic salt
- 1/4 teaspoon pepper
- 1/4 teaspoon anise seed
- 1 1/2 pounds lean ground beef
- 1/2 cup shredded part-skim mozzarella cheese
- 6 hamburger buns split
- 6 lettuce leaves
- 6 tomato slices

Directions

In a large bowl, combine the first six ingredients. Crumble beef over mixture; mix well. Shape into six patties. Place on a broiler pan coated with nonstick cooking spray. Broil 6 in. from heat for 5-6 minutes on each side or until juices run clear. Sprinkle with cheese.

Broil 1-minute longer or until cheese is melted. Serve on buns with lettuce and tomato.

Avocado, Asiago and Prosciutto Pizza

Ingredients

- 1 (10 ounces) thin or whole wheat pizza crust or seasoned flatbread crust
- 1 1/2 ounces prosciutto, thinly sliced
- 3 ounces Asiago cheese, crumbled
- 2 tablespoons fresh basil or Italian parsley, chopped
- 2 Chilean Hass avocados Red pepper flakes

Directions

Preheat oven to 425 degrees F. Place pizza crust on a baking sheet. Arrange prosciutto slices evenly over crust. Sprinkle with Asiago and basil. Bake until lightly browned, about 10 minutes. Cut avocados in half, remove the pit and peel. Cut into slices and arrange over top of the pizza. Sprinkle with red pepper flakes.

Ragu Pizza Burgers

Ingredients

- 1 pound ground beef
- 2 cups Ragu® Old World Style® Pasta Sauce
- 1 cup shredded mozzarella cheese
- 1/4 teaspoon salt
- 6 English muffins, split and toasted

Directions

Combine ground beef, 1/2 cup pasta sauce, 1/2 cup cheese, and salt in a small bowl. Shape into 6 patties. Grill or broil until done.

Meanwhile, heat the remaining Sauce. To serve, arrange burgers on muffin halves. Top with remaining cheese, sauce, and muffin halves.

Appetizer Crab Pizza

Ingredients

- 3 cups all-purpose flour
- 1 (.25 ounce) package active dry yeast
- 1 teaspoon sugar
- 1/2 teaspoon salt
- 1 cup water
- 2 tablespoons olive oil or vegetable oil

TOPPING:

- 2 (8 ounce) packages cream cheese, softened
- 2 (6 ounce) cans crabmeat - drained, flaked, and cartilage removed
- 1/4 cup milk
- 1 cup crumbled feta cheese
- 1 teaspoon dried basil
- 1 teaspoon dried oregano
- 1/2 teaspoon garlic powder
- 1 cup shredded Swiss cheese, divided

Directions

In a large mixing bowl, combine 1-1/2 cups flour, yeast, sugar, and salt. In a saucepan, heat water and oil to 120 degrees F-130 degrees F. Add to dry ingredients; beat on medium speed for 3 minutes. Stir in enough remaining flour to form a soft dough. Turn onto a floured surface; knead until smooth and elastic, about 8 minutes. Place in a greased bowl, turning once to grease top. Cover and let rise in a warm place until doubled, about 1 hour.

Punch dough down; divide in half. On a floured surface, roll each piece into a 13-in. circle; transfer to two 12-in. pizza pans. Build up edge slightly. Prick dough thoroughly with a fork. Bake crusts at 450 degrees F for 10-12 minutes or until lightly browned. Combine the cream cheese, crab, milk, feta cheese, basil, oregano, and garlic powder; spread mixture over each crust. Sprinkle each with 1/2 cup Swiss cheese. Bake 10-12 minutes longer or until crust is golden and cheese is melted. Cut into wedges.

Chicken, Herb and Garlic Pizza with Balsamic

Ingredients

- 1 (11 ounces) package TysonB® Grilled and Readyв" Fully Cooked Grilled Chicken Breast Strips
- 1/4 teaspoon salt
- 1/4 teaspoon pepper 1 tablespoon olive oil
- 1 (10 ounces) refrigerated pizza crust
- 1 (4 ounces) package salad greens
- 3 tablespoons balsamic vinaigrette dressing
- 1 (6.5 ounce) package garlic and herbs cheese spread

Directions

Preheat oven to 450 degrees F. Wash hands. Spread dough on the greased baking sheet into an 11 x 15-inch rectangle—Bake 10 to 12 minutes or until crisp and deep golden brown. When the crust is done, transfer to a cutting board—cool 1 minute; spread with cheese.

Cook chicken according to package directions. Toss salad greens with dressing.

Scrambled Pizza

Ingredients

- 2/3 cup warm water
- 1 (.25 ounce) package instant yeast
- 1/2 teaspoon salt
- 1 teaspoon white sugar
- 1/4 teaspoon dried oregano
- 1 3/4 cups all-purpose flour
- 6 slices bacon, chopped
- 1/2 cup green onion, thinly sliced
- 6 eggs, beaten
- salt and pepper to taste
- 1/2 cup pizza sauce
- 1/4 cup grated Parmesan cheese
- 2 ounces thinly sliced salami

Directions

Preheat oven to 400 degrees F (200 degrees C).

Pour warm water into a mixing bowl. Stir in yeast, salt, sugar, and oregano. Mix in 1 cup flour, and then stir in the remaining flour. Cover with plastic wrap and set aside to rest for 10 to 15 minutes.

While the dough is resting, prepare the topping. Place bacon in a large, deep skillet. Cook over medium heat until evenly brown. Stir in green onions and cook for 1 minute. Add eggs to the pan; cook, frequently stirring, until mixture has the consistency of scrambled eggs—season with salt and pepper to taste.

Spread dough out evenly onto a lightly greased pizza tray and spread pizza sauce over dough. Top with bacon and eggs, Parmesan cheese, and salami.

Bake for 20 to 25 minutes, or until golden brown on top.

Thick Chewy Pizza

Ingredients

- 1 (.25 ounce) package active dry yeast
- 1/4 cup warm water (105 degrees to 115 degrees)
- 1 egg
- 1 (8 ounces) can tomato sauce, divided
- 3 tablespoons vegetable oil
- 1 tablespoon sugar
- 1 teaspoon salt
- 1/4 teaspoon chili powder
- 1/4 teaspoon hot pepper sauce, divided
- 2 1/4 cups all-purpose flour 1 pound ground beef
- 3/4 cup chopped onion
- 1 (4 ounces) can mushroom stems and pieces, drained
- 1/3 cup chopped stuffed olives
- 1/4 cup chopped green pepper 1 tablespoon butter, melted
- 2 cups shredded mozzarella cheese

Directions

In a large mixing bowl, dissolve yeast in warm water. Add egg, 1/4 cup tomato sauce, oil, sugar, salt, chili powder, and 1/8 to 1/4 teaspoon hot pepper sauce; beat until smooth. Add 1 cup flour; beat for 1 minute. Stir in enough remaining flour to form a soft dough.

Turn onto a floured surface; knead until smooth and elastic, about 6-8 minutes. Place in a greased bowl, turning once to grease top. Cover and let rise in a warm place until doubled, about 1 hour.

Meanwhile, in a large skillet, cook beef over medium heat until no longer pink; drain. Remove from the heat; stir in onion, mushrooms, olives, green pepper, and remaining tomato sauce and hot pepper sauce.

Punch dough down; turn once onto a lightly floured surface. Roll into a 14-in. x 9-in. rectangle. Place in a greased 15-in. x 10-in. x 1- in. baking pan. Brush with butter. Top with meat mixture; sprinkle with cheese. Bake at 425 degrees F for 15 minutes or until crust is lightly browned and cheese is melted.

Lahmacun (Armenian Pizza)

Ingredients

- 1-pound lean ground lamb
- 1 1/2 cups finely chopped onion
- 1/2 cup chopped green bell pepper
- 1 teaspoon minced garlic
- 1 (14.5 ounces) can of peeled and diced tomatoes
- 1 (6 ounces) can tomato paste
- 1/2 cup chopped fresh Italian parsley
- 1 teaspoon chopped fresh basil
- 1 tablespoon chopped fresh mint leaves
- 1/2 teaspoon ground cumin
- 1 pinch cayenne pepper (optional)
- 4 pita bread or fluffy tortillas

Directions

Place ground lamb in a large skillet over medium-high heat. Cook and break into small pieces until mostly browned. Drain any excess grease. Add the onion, green pepper, and garlic. Cook until the onion is translucent.

Stir in diced tomatoes and tomato paste, then season with parsley, basil, mint, cumin, and if using, cayenne. Simmer for about 5 minutes. Remove from heat, cover, and refrigerate overnight to blend the flavors.

Preheat the oven to 450 degrees F (230 degrees C). Distribute the lamb mixture evenly over the tortillas and spread out to the edges. Place the tortillas onto a baking sheet.

Bake for about 20 minutes in the preheated oven. Remove from the oven and place the lahmacuns onto a large piece of aluminum foil so that two of them are meat side to meat side, then stack the pairs together and bring the foil up over the top to keep warm. These can be served hot or cold. Cut into small wedges.

Italian Pesto Pizza

Ingredients

- 1 (10 ounces) container refrigerated pizza crust
- 1/2 cup pesto
- 6 ounces marinated fresh mozzarella cheese, sliced
- 1/2 cup prosciutto
- 1/4 cup chopped fresh parsley
- 1tablespoons chopped fresh basil
- 3 tablespoons grated Parmesan cheese

Directions

Preheat oven to 400 degrees F (200 degrees C).

Roll out pizza dough as directed on the package. Spread the pesto evenly on the crust. Arrange mozzarella slices over the pesto; scatter prosciutto over the mozzarella. Sprinkle pizza with fresh parsley, fresh basil, and grated Parmesan. Bake in the preheated oven until crust is browned and pizza is hot and bubbly for about 10 minutes.

White and Gold Pizza

Ingredients

- 3 tablespoons olive oil, divided
- 1 large, sweet onion, thinly sliced, separated into rings
- 1-pound frozen pizza dough, thawed
- 1 large clove garlic, minced
- 4 ounces PHILADELPHIA Cream Cheese, softened
- 3/4 cup KRAFT Shredded Mozzarella Cheese
- 1/2 cup DIGIORNO Grated Romano Cheese
- 1/2 teaspoon crushed red pepper

Directions

Heat oven to 425 degrees F.

Heat 1 Tbsp. Oil in large skillet on medium heat. Add onions; cook 15 to 20 min. Or until tender and golden brown, stirring occasionally.

Place pizza dough on a lightly floured baking sheet; stretch to fit 16 x 12-inch baking sheet. Mix garlic and remaining oil; spread onto dough—Bake 10 min.

Spread crust with cream cheese; top with remaining cheeses, onions, and red pepper. Bake 10 to 12 min. or until crust is lightly browned.

Bacon Cheeseburger Upside Down Pizza

Ingredients

- 8 slices bacon
- 1 pound ground beef
- 1 onion, chopped
- 1 green bell pepper, chopped
- 1 1/2 cups pizza sauce
- 3 roma (plum) tomatoes, chopped
- 4 ounces shredded Cheddar cheese
- 2 eggs
- 1 cup milk
- 1 tablespoon vegetable oil
- 1 cup all-purpose flour
- 1/4 teaspoon salt

Directions

Place bacon in a large, deep skillet. Cook over medium-high heat until evenly brown; drain. Crumble and set aside 2 slices. Crumble the remaining 6 pieces.

Preheat oven to 400 degrees F (200 degrees C).

In a large saucepan over medium-high heat, saute the beef, onion, and bell pepper until beef is browned. Drain, and stir in the 6 slices of crumbled bacon and pizza sauce. Spoon mixture into an ungreased 9x13 inch pan. Sprinkle with tomatoes and top with cheese.

In a medium bowl, beat the eggs slightly. Mix in milk and oil, then add the flour and salt. Beat for 2 minutes at medium speed. Pour evenly over the meat mixture. Sprinkle with the remaining bacon.

Bake in preheated oven for 20 to 30 minutes, or until topping is lightly puffed and deep, golden brown.

Deep-Dish Spaghetti Pizza

Ingredients

- 8 ounces spaghetti, cooked and drained
- 2 slices shredded mozzarella cheese
- 2 eggs, slightly beaten 1 teaspoon salt
- 1/4 teaspoon ground black pepper
- 1 (26 ounces) jar Ragu® Old World Style® Pasta Sauce

Directions

Preheat oven to 375 degrees F. Combine spaghetti, eggs, 1/2 cup cheese, salt, and pepper in a large bowl. Evenly spread into greased 13 x 9-inch baking dish. Evenly top with Pasta Sauce, then remaining cheese.

Bake 35 minutes or until bubbling. Let stand 5 minutes before serving.

Pizza Casserole

Ingredients

- 2 cups uncooked egg noodles
- 1/2-pound lean ground beef
- onion, chopped
- cloves garlic, minced
- 1 green bell pepper, chopped
- 1 cup sliced pepperoni sausage
- 16 ounces pizza sauce
- tablespoons milk
- 1 cup shredded mozzarella cheese

Directions

Preheat oven to 350 degrees F (175 degrees C). Cook noodles according to package directions.

In a medium skillet over medium-high heat, brown the ground beef with onion, garlic, and green bell pepper. Drain excess fat. Stir in the noodles, pepperoni, pizza sauce, and milk, and mix well. Pour this mixture into a 2-quart casserole dish.

Bake at 350 degrees F (175 degrees C) for 20 minutes, top with the cheese, then bake for 5 to 10 more minutes.

Chicken Ranch Pizza with Bacon

Ingredients

- 1 (10.75 ounces) can Campbell'sB® Condensed Cream of Chicken Soup (Regular or 98% Fat-Free)
- 1 (12 inches) prepared thin pizza crust
- 1 (4.5 ounces) can SwansonB® Premium Chunk Chicken Breast in Water, drained
- 1 cup shredded mozzarella cheese
- 1 cup shredded Mexican cheese blend
- 8 slices bacon, cooked and crumbled
- ranch salad dressing

Directions

Heat the oven to 375 degrees F.

Spread the soup onto the pizza crust to within 1/4-inch of the edge. Top with the chicken, cheeses, and bacon. Bake for 10 minutes or until the cheese is melted and the crust is golden.

Drizzle the ranch dressing over the pizza.

Smoked Salmon Pizzas

Ingredients

- 6 (6 inches) pita bread
- 1/4 cup pizza sauce
- 1/4-pound smoked salmon, chopped
- 1 small red onion, halved and thinly sliced
- 1 cup shredded mozzarella cheese
- 1/4 teaspoon dried oregano

Directions

Place pitas on an ungreased baking sheet. Top with pizza sauce, salmon, onion, cheese, and oregano. Bake at 425 degrees F for 7-10 minutes or until cheese is melted.

Baked Potato Pizza

Ingredients

- 1 (6.5 ounces) package pizza crust mix
- 3 medium unpeeled potatoes, baked and cooled
- 1 tablespoon butter or margarine, melted
- 1/4 teaspoon garlic powder
- 1/4 teaspoon dried Italian seasoning
- 1 cup sour cream
- 6 bacon strips, cooked and crumbled
- 3 green onions, chopped
- 1 1/2 cups shredded mozzarella cheese
- 1/2 cup shredded Cheddar cheese

Directions

Prepare crust according to package directions. Press dough into a lightly greased 14-in. pizza pan; build up edges slightly. Bake at 400 degrees F for 5-6 minutes or until crust is firm and begins to brown.

Cut potatoes into 1/2-in. Cubes. In a bowl, combine butter, garlic powder, and Italian seasoning. Add potatoes and toss—spread sour cream over crust; top with potato mixture, bacon, onions, and cheeses. Bake at 400 degrees F for 15-20 minutes or until cheese is lightly browned. Let stand for 5 minutes before cutting.

Deluxe Turkey Club Pizza

Ingredients

- 1 (10 ounces) refrigerated pizza crust
- 1 tablespoon sesame seeds
- 1/4 cup mayonnaise
- 1teaspoon grated lemon peel
- 1 medium tomato, thinly sliced
- 1/2 cup cubed cooked turkey
- 4 bacon strips, cooked and crumbled
- 2medium fresh mushrooms, thinly sliced
- 1/4 cup chopped onion
- 1 1/2 cups shredded Colby- Monterey Jack cheese

Directions

Unroll pizza dough and press onto a greased 12-in. pizza pan; build up edges slightly. Sprinkle with sesame seeds. Bake at 425 degrees F for 12-14 minutes or until edges are lightly browned.

Combine mayonnaise and lemon peel; spread over crust. Top with tomato, turkey, bacon, mushrooms, onion, and cheese. Bake for 6-8 minutes or until cheese is melted. Cut into slices.

Crab-Artichoke Pizza

Ingredients

- 1-pound fresh pizza dough
- 1/4 teaspoon red pepper flakes
- 1 (6 ounces) can crabmeat - drained, and cartilage removed
- 1(6 ounces) jar quartered artichoke hearts in water, drained
- 2tablespoons olive oil
- 1 1/2 tablespoons minced garlic
- 1/2 cup shredded Parmesan cheese
- 1 cup shredded mozzarella cheese

Directions

Preheat oven to 350 degrees F (175 degrees C). Lightly grease a pizza pan.

Roll out pizza dough on a floured surface to a 14 or 16-inch circle; place onto a pizza pan. Sprinkle dough with red pepper flakes, then top evenly with crab and artichokes. Drizzle with olive oil, then sprinkle with garlic, Parmesan cheese, and mozzarella cheese.

Bake in the preheated oven until the cheese has melted and the crust is no longer doughy about 20 minutes. Set oven to broil and cook pizza for 5 minutes more until the cheese has begun to brown.

Cheese-Stuffed Hawaiian Pizza

Ingredients

- 2 (10 inches) flour tortillas
- 1 1/2 cups shredded part-skim mozzarella cheese, divided
- 1/4 cup pizza sauce
- 1/2 cup pineapple tidbits, drained
- 3/4 cup diced fully cooked ham

Directions

Place one tortilla on a baking sheet coated with nonstick cooking spray. Sprinkle with 1 cup cheese. Top with the second tortilla; spread with pizza sauce. Sprinkle with pineapple, ham, and remaining cheese. Bake at 375 degrees F for 15 minutes or until tortillas are crisp and cheese is melted.

Peppery Pizza Loaves

Ingredients

- 1 1/2 pounds ground beef
- 1/2 teaspoon garlic powder
- 1/2 teaspoon salt
- 2 (8 ounces) loaves of French bread, halved lengthwise
- 1 (8 ounces) jar process cheese sauce
- 1 (4 ounces) can mushroom stems and pieces, drained
- 1 cup chopped green onions
- 1 (4 ounces) can slice jalapeno peppers, drained
- 1 (8 ounces) can tomato sauce
- 1/2 cup grated Parmesan cheese
- 4 cups shredded mozzarella cheese

Directions

In a skillet, cook beef over medium heat until no longer pink; drain. Stir in garlic powder and salt. Place each bread half on a large piece of heavy-duty foil. Spread with cheese sauce. Top with beef mixture, mushrooms, onions, and jalapenos. Drizzle with tomato sauce. Top with Parmesan and mozzarella cheeses. Wrap and freeze. It may be frozen for up to 3 months. To bake: Unwrap loaves and thaw on baking sheets in the refrigerator. Bake at 350 degrees F for 18 minutes or until cheese is melted.

Smoked Salmon Pizza

Ingredients

- 1 (12 inches) prebaked pizza crust
- 1 tablespoon olive oil
- cup smoked salmon, cut into
- 1/2-inch pieces
- 1/2 (6 ounces) jar marinated artichoke hearts, drained and quartered
- tablespoons chopped sun-dried tomatoes
- cups shredded mozzarella cheese

Directions

Preheat an oven to 400 degrees F (200 degrees C).

Spread the olive oil over the pizza crust, then sprinkle with the smoked salmon, artichokes, and sun-dried tomatoes. Sprinkle the mozzarella cheese evenly over the pizza.

Bake in the preheated oven until the cheese has melted and is bubbly, 10 to 15 minutes.

Gourmet White Pizza

Ingredients

- 2tablespoons butter melted 1 tablespoon olive oil
- 3tablespoons minced garlic
- 2 tablespoons sun-dried tomato pesto
- 1 teaspoon dried basil
- 1 teaspoon dried oregano
- 1 tablespoon grated Parmesan cheese
- 1cup Alfredo sauce
- 2cups chopped cooked chicken breast meat
- 1 (12 inches) prebaked pizza crust
- 1 medium tomato, sliced
- 1 (4 ounces) package feta cheese

Directions

Preheat the oven to 375 degrees F (190 degrees C).

In a small bowl, mix together the butter, olive oil, garlic, pesto, basil, oregano, Parmesan cheese, and Alfredo sauce. Arrange the chicken on top of the pizza crust.

Pour the Alfredo sauce mixture evenly over the chicken. Top with tomato and feta cheese.

Bake for 10 to 15 minutes in the preheated oven until the crust is lightly browned and toppings are toasted. Cut into wedges to serve.

Pizza Roll-Ups

Ingredients

- 1/2-pound ground beef
- 1 (8 ounces) can tomato sauce
- 1/2 cup shredded mozzarella cheese
- 1/2 teaspoon dried oregano
- 2 (8 ounce) cans refrigerated crescent rolls

Directions

In a skillet, cook beef over medium heat until no longer pink; drain. Remove from the heat.

Add tomato sauce, mozzarella cheese, and oregano; mix well.

Separate crescent dough into eight rectangles, pinching seams together. Place about 3 tablespoons of meat mixture along one long side of each rectangle. Roll up, jelly-roll style, starting with a long side. Cut each roll into three pieces: place, seam side down, 2 in. apart on greased baking sheets.

Bake at 375 degrees for 15 minutes or until golden brown.

Pizza Pasta Bake

Ingredients

- 1 (12 ounces) package uncooked elbow macaroni
- 1/2-pound mild Italian sausage
- 1/2 cup chopped onion
- 1 (14 ounces) pizza sauce
- 1 (8 ounces) tomato sauce
- 1/2 cup milk
- 1 (3.25 ounce) package sliced pepperoni, cut in half
- 1/4 cup sliced fresh mushrooms
- 1/4 cup sliced black olives
- 1/4 cup chopped Canadian bacon
- 1 cup shredded mozzarella cheese

Directions

Preheat oven to 350 degrees F (175 degrees C).

Bring a large pot of lightly salted water to a boil. Stir in macaroni, cook for 8 to 10 minutes, until al dente, and drain.

In a skillet over medium heat, cook the Italian sausage and onion until the sausage is evenly brown and onion is tender—drain grease.

In a bowl, mix the pizza sauce, tomato sauce, and milk. Stir in the sausage and onion, pepperoni, mushrooms, olives, and Canadian bacon. Gently mix in the cooked macaroni until evenly coated.

Transfer to the prepared baking dish.

Cover, and bake for 30 minutes in the preheated oven. Remove cover, top with cheese, and continue baking for 15 minutes until cheese is melted and bubbly.

Cheese Steak Pizza

Ingredients

- 1 (8 ounces) package refrigerated crescent rolls
- 1medium green pepper, chopped
- 1 medium onion, chopped
- 1/4 teaspoon beef bouillon granules
- 2tablespoons olive oil
- 1/2 pound thinly sliced deli roast beef
- 1 tablespoon Italian salad dressing
- 1 1/2 cups shredded mozzarella cheese

Directions

Unroll crescent roll dough and place in an ungreased 13-in. x 9-in. x 2-in. baking pan. Press onto the bottom and 1/2 in. up the sides to form a crust; seal perforations. Bake at 375 degrees F for 7-10 minutes or until lightly browned.

Meanwhile, in a large skillet, saute the green pepper, onion, and bouillon in oil until vegetables are tender; set aside. Arrange beef over crust. Brush with salad dressing and sprinkle with mozzarella cheese. Bake 4-5 minutes longer or until cheese is melted. Top with green pepper mixture. Cut into squares.

Crab and Pineapple Pizza

Ingredients

- 2 (10 ounces) cans of refrigerated pizza dough
- 2 (6 ounce) cans crabmeat, drained and flaked
- 1 cup canned pizza sauce
- 1 (8 ounces) can pineapple chunks, drained and roughly chopped
- 1 (8 ounces) package light cream cheese, cubed

Directions

Preheat the oven to 400 degrees F (200 degrees C). Grease a pizza pan or cookie sheet.

Spread both cans of dough out to cover the prepared pan, sealing any seams. Spread a thin layer of pizza sauce over the crust, and dot with cream cheese cubes. Sprinkle shredded crabmeat over, then pineapple pieces.

Bake for 12 to 15 minutes in the preheated oven until the crust is lightly browned.

Thai Chicken Pizza

Ingredients

- 1 (12 inches) prebaked pizza crust
- 1 (7 ounces) jar peanut sauce
- 1/4 cup peanut butter
- 8 ounces cooked skinless, boneless chicken breast halves, cut into strips
- 1 cup shredded Italian cheese blend
- 1 bunch green onions, chopped
- 1/2 cup fresh bean sprouts (optional)
- 1/2 cup shredded carrot (optional)
- 1 tablespoon chopped roasted peanuts (optional)

Directions

Preheat the oven to 400 degrees F (200 degrees C).

In a small bowl, stir together the peanut sauce and peanut butter. Spread over the pizza crust. Arrange strips of chicken on top.

Sprinkle on the green onions and cheese.

Bake for 8 to 12 minutes in the preheated oven until cheese is melted and bubbly. Top with bean sprouts, carrot shreds, and peanuts if using. Slice into wedges and serve.

Thai Chicken Pizza with Carrots and Cilantro

Ingredients

- 1(12 inches) prebaked Italian pizza crust
- 1/2 cup prepared Thai peanut sauce
- 2tablespoons peanut butter
- 2 cups shredded chicken
- 2medium carrots, peeled and grated
- 3green onions, thinly sliced
- 1/4 cup chopped roasted peanuts
- 1/4 cup chopped fresh cilantro

Directions

Adjust oven rack to lowest position, and heat oven to 450 degrees—place crust on a cookie sheet. Mix peanut sauce and peanut butter, then spread 2/3 of the sauce over the pizza crust; toss remaining 1/3 of the sauce with the shredded chicken—spread chicken over pizza.

Bake until the crust is crisp and golden, 10 to 12 minutes. Remove from oven, and top with carrots, green onions, peanuts, and cilantro. Cut into 6 slices and serve.

Brunch Pizza Squares

Ingredients

- 1 pound bulk pork sausage
- 1 (8 ounces) can refrigerated crescent rolls
- 4 eggs
- 2 tablespoons milk
- 1/8 teaspoon pepper
- 3/4 cup shredded Cheddar cheese

Directions

In a skillet, cook sausage over medium heat until no longer pink; drain. Unroll crescent dough into a lightly greased 13-in. x 9-in. x 2- in. baking pan. Press dough 1/2 in. up the sides; seal seams.

Sprinkle with sausage. In a bowl, beat the eggs, milk, and pepper; pour over sausage. Sprinkle with cheese.

Bake, uncovered, at 400 degrees for 15 minutes or until the crust is golden brown and the cheese is melted.

Pizza Sauce and Dough

Ingredients

PIZZA DOUGH:

- 1/4 cup warm water (100 to 110 degrees)
- 1 teaspoon active dry yeast
- 1 teaspoon white sugar
- 4 cups bread flour
- 2 tablespoons Italian-style seasoning
- 1 teaspoon salt, divided
- 1 1/4 cups flat beer
- 1tablespoon olive oil

PIZZA SAUCE:

- 2tablespoons olive oil
- 1/3 cup chopped onion
- 2 tablespoons chopped garlic
- 1(28 ounces) can roma tomatoes, with juice
- 2(6 ounce) cans tomato paste
- 1 tablespoon chopped fresh basil
- 1 tablespoon chopped fresh parsley

- 1 teaspoon chopped fresh oregano
- 1/2 teaspoon black pepper

Directions

In a small bowl, dissolve yeast and sugar in warm water. Let stand until creamy, about 10 minutes.

In a food processor, combine flour, Italian seasoning, and salt. Pulse until mixed. Add yeast mixture, flat beer, and oil. Pulse until a ball is formed. Scrape the dough out onto a lightly floured surface and knead for several minutes until the dough is smooth and elastic. Allow dough to rest for 2 to 3 minutes. Divide dough in half, and shape into balls. Place dough balls in separate bowls and cover with plastic wrap.

Allow to rise at room temperature for about 1 hour, then store in the refrigerate overnight.

To make the sauce: Heat olive oil in a saucepan over medium heat. Saute onions until tender. Stir in garlic and cook for 1 minute.

Crush tomatoes into a saucepan. Add tomato paste, basil, parsley, and oregano. Simmer for 10 minutes.

Mexican Pizza

Ingredients

- 1/2-pound ground beef
- 1 medium onion, diced
- 1 clove garlic, minced
- 1 tablespoon chili powder
- 1 teaspoon ground cumin
- 1/2 teaspoon paprika
- 1/2 teaspoon black pepper
- 1/2 teaspoon salt
- 1 (16 ounces) can refried beans
- 4 (10 inches) flour tortillas
- 1/2 cup salsa
- 1 cup shredded Cheddar cheese
- 1 cup shredded Monterey Jack cheese
- 2 green onions, chopped
- 2 roma (plum) tomatoes, diced
- 1/4 cup finely chopped jalapeno peppers
- 1/4 cup sour cream (optional)

Directions

Preheat the oven to 350 degrees F (175 degrees C). Coat 2 pie plates with nonstick cooking spray.

Place beef, onion, and garlic in a skillet over medium heat. Cook until beef is evenly browned. Drain off grease. Season the meat with chili powder, cumin, paprika, salt, and pepper.

Lay one tortilla in each pie plate and cover it with a layer of refried beans. Spread half of the seasoned ground beef over each one, and then cover with a second tortilla— Bake for 10 minutes in the preheated oven.

Remove the plates from the oven and let cool slightly. Spread half of the salsa over each top tortilla. Cover each pizza with half of the Cheddar and Monterey Jack cheeses. Place half of the tomatoes, half of the green onions, and half of the jalapeno slices onto each one.

Return the pizzas to the oven, and bake for 5 to 10 more minutes until the cheese is melted. Remove from the oven and let cool slightly before slicing each one into 4 pieces.

BBQ Chicken Pizza

Ingredients

- 1(12 inches) prebaked pizza crust
- 1 cup spicy barbeque sauce
- 2 skinless, boneless chicken breast halves, cooked and cubed
- 1/2 cup chopped fresh cilantro
- 1 cup sliced pepperoncini peppers
- 1 cup chopped red onion
- 2 cups shredded Colby-Monterey Jack cheese

Directions

Preheat oven to 350 degrees F (175 degrees C).

Place pizza crust on a medium baking sheet. Spread the crust with barbeque sauce. Top with chicken, cilantro, pepperoncini peppers, onion, and cheese.

Bake in the preheated oven for 15 minutes or until cheese is melted and bubbly.

Upside-Down Pizza

Ingredients

- 1 pound ground beef
- 2 Italian sausage links, casings removed
- 1 (28 ounces) jar spaghetti sauce with meat
- 1/2 cup pizza sauce
- 4 ounces sliced pepperoni
- 1 (16 ounces) package shredded pizza cheese blend
- 1 (13.8 ounces) refrigerated pizza crust

Directions

Preheat oven to 450 degrees F (230 degrees C).

Heat a large skillet over medium-high heat and stir in the ground beef and Italian sausage. Cook and stir until the meat is crumbly, evenly browned, and no longer pink; drain. Stir in the spaghetti sauce, pizza sauce, and pepperoni, and heat until bubbly. Transfer the mixture to an 11x13 inch baking dish.

Sprinkle evenly with the shredded pizza cheese. Top with the pizza dough.

Bake in the preheated oven until crust is lightly browned, about 20 minutes.

Grilled Mediterranean Greek Pizza

Ingredients

- 1 (12 ounces) package al fresco® All-Natural Sun-Dried Tomato with Basil Chicken Sausage
- 1 (14 ounces) package baked pizza crust (such as Boboli)
- 2 tablespoons garlic-flavored olive oil
- 2/3 cup pizza sauce
- 1 cup shredded Italian cheese blend, reduced fat
- 1/3 cup crumbled feta cheese with basil and tomato
- 1 1/2 teaspoons dried oregano

Directions

Preheat grill on medium setting.

Place sausages on an oiled grill rack set 4 to 5 inches overheat. Grill, using the direct grill method, turning links with tongs, until cooked throughout, about 7 to 9 minutes or until the internal temperature reaches 165 degrees F. Cool slightly and cut into 1/4 to 1/2-inch slices.

Brush both sides of the pizza crust with olive oil. Gently place pizza crust, top-side down on grill rack. Grill for 2 to 3 minutes until the crust is warm. Turn crust over.

Quickly spread pizza sauce on the cooked side of pizza crust, then arrange sliced sausage on top of the crust. Sprinkle with cheese and oregano—grill over direct medium heat. Cover with grill lid or tent with foil.

Grill for 8 to 10 minutes or until toppings are warm and cheese has melted. Cut into wedges and serve.

Chicken and Cranberry Pizza with Brie

Ingredients

- 1 (12 inches) prebaked Italian pizza crust
- 1 1/2 cups whole-berry cranberry sauce from a 16-ounce can
- 2 cups shredded chicken*
- 4 ounces Brie, cut into small chunks
- 3 green onions, thinly sliced
- 1/4 cup slivered almonds
- 1 cup shredded mozzarella

Directions

Adjust oven rack to lowest position, and heat oven to 450 degrees. Place crust on a cookie sheet and spread 1 cup of cranberry sauce over the crust. Toss remaining 1/2 cup with chicken. Top pizza with chicken, Brie, green onions, almonds, and mozzarella. Bake until the crust is crisp and cheese melts 10 to 12 minutes. Cut into 6 slices and serve.

Pita Pizzas

Ingredients

- 1 pound ground turkey breast
- 1 cup sliced fresh mushrooms
- 1/2 cup chopped onion
- 2 garlic cloves, minced
- 1 (8 ounces) can no-salt-added tomato sauce
- 1/2 teaspoon fennel seed
- 1/4 teaspoon dried oregano
- 4 pita bread, warmed
- 1/2 cup shredded reduced-fat mozzarella cheese

Directions

In a skillet, brown the turkey; drain. Add mushrooms, onion, and garlic; cook until tender. Stir in tomato sauce, fennel seed, and oregano. Cover and simmer for 10-15 minutes or until heated through. Spread 1 cup of meat mixture on each pita; sprinkle with cheese. Serve immediately.

Turkey Tomato Pizza

Ingredients

- 1(10 ounces) refrigerated pizza crust
- 2teaspoons sesame seeds
- 1/4 cup reduced-fat mayonnaise
- 1/4 teaspoon grated lemon peel
- 1 cup (4 ounces) shredded reduced-fat Mexican-blend cheese
- 1 teaspoon dried basil
- 1/4 pound thinly sliced deli turkey, julienned
- 3 bacon strips, cooked and crumbled
- 2 small tomatoes, thinly sliced
- 1cup shredded reduced-fat Swiss cheese
- 2tablespoons thinly sliced green onions

Directions

Unroll the pizza crust onto a 15-in. x 10-in. x 1-in. baking pan coated with nonstick cooking spray. Flatten dough and build-up edges slightly. Prick dough several times with a fork; sprinkle with sesame seeds. Bake at 425 degrees F for 10-12 minutes or until lightly browned.

Combine the mayonnaise and lemon peel; spread over crust. Sprinkle with Mexican or mozzarella cheese and basil. Top with turkey, bacon, tomatoes, and Swiss cheese. Bake for 7-9 minutes or until the crust is golden brown and cheese is melted. Sprinkle with onion.

Pizza Meat Loaf

Ingredients

- 1 envelope Lipton® Recipe Secrets® Beefy Onion Soup Mix
- 2 pounds ground beef
- 1 1/2 cups fresh breadcrumbs
- 2 eggs
- 1 small green bell pepper, chopped (optional)
- 1/4 cup water
- 1 cup Ragu® Old World Style® Pasta Sauce
- 1 cup shredded mozzarella cheese

Directions

Preheat oven to 350 degrees F. Combine all ingredients except 1/2 cup Pasta Sauce and 1/2 cup cheese in a large bowl.

Shape into loaf in 13 x 9-inch baking or roasting pan. Top with remaining 1/2 cup Sauce. Bake 50 minutes. Sprinkle top with remaining 1/2 cup cheese. Bake an additional 10 minutes or until done. Let stand 10 minutes before serving.

Husband-Friendly Chicken Pizza

Ingredients

- 1/4 cup olive oil
- 1 red onion, sliced
- 6 slices bacon
- 1(10 ounces) container refrigerated pizza crust
- 3/4 cup barbeque sauce
- 2cooked chicken breast halves, shredded
- 1/4 cup crumbled Gorgonzola cheese
- 1 jalapeno pepper, seeded and diced, or to taste (optional)
- 1 tablespoon paprika
- 1 tablespoon garlic powder
- 2 cups shredded mozzarella cheese

Directions

Heat the oil in a skillet over medium heat. Stir in the onion; cook and stir until the onion has softened and turned translucent for about 5 minutes. Reduce heat to medium-low and continue cooking and stirring until the onion is very tender and dark brown, 15 to 20 minutes more.

Place the bacon in a large, deep skillet, and cook over medium-high heat, occasionally turning, until evenly browned, about 10 minutes. Drain the bacon slices on a paper towel-lined plate; crumble when cool.

Preheat an oven to 425 degrees F (220 degrees C). Grease a baking sheet.

Press the refrigerated pizza crust onto the baking sheet to fit the size of the pan. Spread the barbeque sauce evenly over the dough, and sprinkle with the shredded chicken, caramelized onion, bacon, Gorgonzola cheese, and diced jalapeno pepper. Season with paprika and garlic powder. Top with the shredded mozzarella cheese.

Bake in the preheated oven until the cheese has melted and is bubbly, and the pizza dough is golden brown on the bottom, 15 to 17 minutes.

CPSIA information can be obtained
at www.ICGtesting.com
Printed in the USA
BVHW060439250321
603396BV00004B/276

9 781802 238716